VOICES OF WAR

The Persian Gulf War
War Against Iraqi Aggression

Enzo George

Cavendish
Square
New York

Published in 2015 by Cavendish Square Publishing, LLC
243 5th Avenue, Suite 136, New York, NY 10016

© 2015 Brown Bear Books Ltd

First Edition

Website: cavendishsq.com

CPSIA Compliance Information: Batch #WS14CSQ

All websites were available and accurate when this book was sent to press.

Library of Congress Cataloging-in-Publication Data
George, Enzo.
 The Persian Gulf War : war against Iraqi aggression / Enzo George.
     pages cm _ (Voices of war)
 Includes index.
 ISBN 978-1-62712-876-6 (hardcover) ISBN 978-1-62712-878-0 (ebook)
 1. Persian Gulf War, 1991_Juvenile literature. I. Title.

 DS79.723.B43 2015
 956.7044'2_dc23

                    2014010690

For Brown Bear Books Ltd:
Editorial Director: Lindsey Lowe
Managing Editor: Tim Cooke
Children's Publisher: Anne O'Daly
Design Manager: Keith Davis
Designer: Lynne Lennon
Picture Manager: Sophie Mortimer
Production Director: Alastair Gourlay

CONTENTS

Introduction

I raq invaded its neighbor Kuwait, at the head of the Persian Gulf, in August 1990. That left the Iraqi dictator Saddam Hussein in charge of over a quarter of the world's oil supplies. At the United Nations (UN), many countries condemned the invasion. Arab nations in particular feared upheaval in the Middle East.

When Hussein ignored UN orders to leave Kuwait, the United States organized a coalition of 34 UN members to send forces and support to the Gulf. In Operation Desert Shield, some 750,000 troops arrived in the region, mainly in Saudi Arabia. They prepared to take on the Iraqis. The Iraqi army was huge and it was feared that the Iraqis might use chemical or biological weapons.

A B-52 Stratofortress sets out for a bombing raid on targets in Iraq during the six-week air campaign.

U.S. soldiers get used to wearing protective gear in case of chemical attack.

U.S. soldiers patrol through the desert in a Humvee with a machine gun mounted on the roof.

In January 1991, the Coalition began an air campaign against Iraq. It struck military and strategic targets and also used long-range missiles fired from warships sailing in the Gulf. The Iraqis fired Scud missiles at Coalition forces, but most were harmlessly shot down.

On February 24, 1991, Coalition commanders launched Operation Desert Storm, a land invasion of Kuwait. Demoralized Iraqi soldiers quickly fled, setting fire to Kuwaiti oil wells as they left. The fighting was over after just three days. U.S. President George H. W. Bush did not want to continue the war into Iraq. Saddam Hussein remained in power. He would clash again with the Americans just 12 years later.

Going to War

The invasion of Kuwait left Iraqi dictator Saddam Hussein in control of over a quarter of the world's oil reserves.

On August 2, 1990, Iraq invaded its neighbor, Kuwait. Iraq now controlled over a quarter of the world's oil reserves. On behalf of the United Nations (UN) the United States put together an international coalition to oppose Iraq. In less than six weeks around 120,000 U.S. soldiers were in Saudi Arabia as part of Operation Desert Shield. Another 30,000 waited on ships in the Persian Gulf.

A column of Iraqi tanks rolls into Kuwait City. The Iraqis easily overcame their tiny neighbor.

" This conflict started August 2nd when the dictator of Iraq invaded a small and helpless neighbor. Kuwait—a member of the Arab League and a member of the United Nations—was crushed; its people, brutalized. Five months ago, Saddam Hussein started this cruel war against Kuwait. Tonight, the battle has been joined.

This military action, taken in accord with United Nations resolutions and with the consent of the United States Congress, follows months of constant and virtually endless diplomatic activity on the part of the United Nations, the United States, and many, many other countries…

Now the twenty-eight countries with forces in the Gulf area have exhausted all reasonable efforts to reach a peaceful resolution—[we] have no choice but to drive Saddam from Kuwait by force. We will not fail. **"**

President George Bush addresses the nation on January 19, 1991, when the bombing of Iraq began.

GOING TO WAR FACTS

- During Operation Desert Shield around 500,000 U.S. troops arrived in the Persian Gulf, mainly in Saudi Arabia.
- More than 250,000 Coalition soldiers were also in Saudi Arabia, from UN members including Britain, France, and the Arab countries.
- Saddam Hussein was thought to possess both chemical and biological weapons.
- The Soviet Union sent no troops but did not block the United Nations' decision to go to war against Saddam Hussein.
- The war was notable for new weapons technology, including the Stealth bomber and the Patriot cruise missile.

Recruitment and Training

The Iraqis had around a million soldiers, so the Coalition needed to raise a large army. For the first time since the Vietnam War (1959-1973), U.S. reservists were called into military service. Like regular military personnel, the reservists had to be trained for the possibility of facing chemical or biological weapons, both of which Iraq was believed to possess.

Men from 25th Infantry Division defend their position in a training exercise before heading to the Gulf.

U.S. Marine recruits hold up their rifles during a physical training session at their base in San Diego .

> " At that time, I was a captain in the reserves in armored. I had changed branches again and got armored… I retired as an armored captain. But we had to go. That was a big thing, and everything this time was done by the steps. It wasn't nothing, like you say, haphazardly like it was in Nam and these other wars. We did it by the book.…
>
> At that time I was at Fort Knox, so we had a certain time period to get our weapons to Knox, our tanks loaded on boxcars or flatcars. The worst part there was sitting and waiting after we got there. Of course while we were waiting, we had to go through all these simulators and get retrained for the [desert] environment. "

Kenneth Kay Rodgers had served in the Vietnam War. He was in the reserves when Operation Desert Storm took place and served again, over 20 years later.

RECRUITMENT FACTS

- More than 140,000 reservists were sent to the Gulf War.
- To prepare for the war, reservists had 55 days dedicated training.
- The Gulf War was the first major war in which the U.S. Army did not use conscription. The people who fought were all volunteers.
- More than 40,000 military women were sent to the Gulf, the largest deployment of women in U.S. military history.
- Soldiers received many inoculations, including controversial anthrax injections, in case the Iraqis used biological weapons.

Weapons and Uniforms

The desert environment of the Persian Gulf placed great demands on soldiers' uniforms and weapons. Everything had to work in extreme heat, dust, and sand. Uniforms also had to be resistant to chemical attack. Military technology had advanced and this was the first war to use long-range weapons that could be fired from hundreds of miles away. More conventional weapons like guns were liable to get jammed with sand. Tanks and Humvees also suffered in the difficult conditions.

A soldier from 101st Airborne Division cleans his M-16A2 rifle at the start of Operation Desert Storm.

❝ Constant focus on the chemical threat required us to conduct two hours of chemical training per day. This consisted of wearing chemical overgarments while performing other tasks. Wearing the ensemble was called MOPP IV, (Mission Oriented Protective Posture Level IV). MOPP IV increased our water consumption considerably, as you could lose a gallon of body fluid from sweating during one hour of wearing the charcoal-lined suit and black rubber gloves, boots, and facemask.

We had to learn to tolerate the uncomfortable conditions before practicing ordinary battle skills as well as tasks related to wearing MOPP IV, such as changing protective filters and drinking water… all those tasks I had despised doing back at Fort Stewart. Now the very possibility of fighting in a chemically contaminated environment had me paying close attention to every step. **❞**

Greg Downey was a first lieutenant, Scouts, Task Force 1-64 Armor, 24th Infantry Division.

EQUIPMENT FACTS

- Desert uniforms were issued with body armor and MOPP (Mission Oriented Protective Posture) suits.
- Soldiers kept gas masks and MOPP suits with them at all times in case of a possible chemical attack.
- MOPP suits had strips of detector paper that changed color in the event of a chemical attack.
- The Patriot ground-to-air missile system was used for the first time. Its range was approx 30 miles (50 km).
- The F-117 stealth fighter jet was used for the first time to bomb Baghdad.

M-1 A1 Abrams tanks test their guns in Saudi Arabia. The flat deserts were ideal terrain for armor.

Life in the Gulf

Big challenges awaited U.S. soldiers in the Gulf. The temperature often hit 120°F (48°C) during the day. The desert was the source of huge sandstorms that covered everything in sand. In Saudi Arabia, soldiers lived in tent cities. Because Saudi Arabia is a Muslim country soldiers had to follow Islamic laws. Women had to cover their hair and arms, and alcohol was forbidden.

Members of 354th Tactical Fighter Wing shop in a store on their base during Operation Desert Shield.

U.S. Marines eat their dinners on Thanksgiving Day in Saudi Arabia in November 1990.

" I spent most of today buffing up our bunker. Barry Gardner and I shored up the wood roof and laid out sandbags while some of the flight nurses filled and tied sandbags. We'll use some of them to wall off our yard before putting in our gravel lawn. Then I built one of the nurses a vanity table out of scrap lumber and plywood.

What's amazing is how everyone has adapted so well to living in tents. Contrast us to the Army group across the street living in villas with private showers and baths and even washing machines. All they do is complain how bad the Army is, while we borrow their washing machine. Right now we're using 30mm shells as barter items. But these are so plentiful that they're losing their marketability… That's why we were out looking for Scud parts.

Liz traded her flight knife… to a guy from the French Air Force who promised her regular Perrier and bread. These guys have their own baker. **"**

Major Bob Munson was an evacuation flight surgeon at King Khalid Military City in Saudi Arabia. He wrote home to tell his family how he passed the time when not working.

LIFE IN THE GULF FACTS

- By the end of September 1990 there were around 120,000 U.S. troops in Saudi Arabia.
- During the first days in Saudi Arabia most men were drinking nearly a liter of water per hour. Hundreds of thousands of gallons of water were flown in.
- U.S. forces were issued with 306,000 bottles of sun cream and 247,000 pairs of special desert sunglasses.
- Soldiers used aluminum cots to sleep on because of the risk from snakes and scorpions on the ground.

Women in the Gulf

Female U.S. miliary personnel are briefed on what to expect when they deploy to Saudi Arabia as part of Operation Desert Shield.

The Gulf War was the first major U.S. conflict in which women served on the front line. They were in support units close to the front. They worked as nurses, clerks, truck drivers, communications specialists, and logistic managers. They piloted Black Hawk helicopters or refueled aircraft. Although they were not supposed to fight, many were involved in front-line action.

WOMEN IN THE GULF FACTS

- More than 40,000 servicewomen went to the Gulf, compared with 7,000 (mainly nurses) who served in Vietnam.
- One out of every five U.S. women in uniform was deployed in direct support to the Gulf War.
- Thirteen U.S. servicewomen were killed during the war.
- Although women were not officially supposed to be involved in combat, in practice the difference between combat and noncombat was often small.
- Two U.S. military women were taken prisoner by the Iraqis but were later released unharmed.

❝ At the front line, first and foremost, you were a soldier. My cot, when I had one, was not always separate from males. We slept in our uniforms. The only way I bathed was with a small blue plastic bucket. I used fresh water to wash myself, and my clothes, and then one bucket of fresh water to rinse. This happened about twice a week. Bathrooms did not exist, except when a hole was dug in the sand and a tarp was placed around it for privacy. The only food I ate was packaged, called 'MREs' (Meals Ready to Eat). They are meant to be heated, but we had no way to warm them up.

When your unit is up front where the battles are, you are expected to be a soldier and do your job. If you don't, it doesn't matter if you are male or female: you will be sent back to the rear with the noncombat troops. **❞**

Captain Lorraine Holland served in the Army Ordnance Corps as part of 498th Support Battalion, 2nd Armored Division.

U.S. soldiers carry water at a base. Women were integrated into almost every U.S. unit in the Gulf.

The Coalition

The United States led a coalition of thirty-four nations. The Coalition had been created on behalf of the United Nations Security Council when it became clear that UN sanctions would not force Iraq to leave Kuwait. Some countries, including Britain and members of the Arab League of Nations, were ready to fight. Others, such as Canada, did not want to be involved in fighting but were prepared to play a support or peacekeeping role.

Egyptian rangers in a Jeep wait to take part in a parade during Operation Desert Shield.

Troops from Britain and other Coalition countries wait to be reviewed by King Fahd of Saudi Arabia.

❝ The government has… accepted the advice of our military staff to have Canadian ships operate within the Persian Gulf. They will be under Canadian command and control and will have responsibility for a sector across the middle of the Gulf… Our ships will be operating in the same general area as the ships of the United States, the United Kingdom and other allied navies… Canadian ships have recently been equipped with their own upgraded air defense capability. They will benefit as well from the combined air defense capabilities of allies in the region…

As a further initiative, the government… decided to deploy a squadron of CF-18 fighter aircraft from Lahr, West Germany, to the Gulf to operate under Canadian control and provide air cover for our own ships and the ships of friendly nations. With supporting elements this will engage up to 450 additional Canadian military personnel in the region. **❞**

Canadian Prime Minister Brian Mulroney addressed Canadians on September 14, 1990, to explain why involvement in the Gulf had become necessary. It was, he said, "Saddam Hussein against the world."

COALITION FACTS

- On August 2, 1990, the United Nations Security Council passed Resolution 990, demanding the withdrawal of Iraqi troops from Kuwait.
- On August 6, 1990, the Security Council passed Resolution 991, imposing sanctions—trade restrictions—on Iraq.
- On August 7, 1990, U.S. forces moved into Saudi Arabia to protect it from possible Iraqi attack.
- The United States remained the largest member of the Coalition.
- Thirty-three other nations sent a combined total of 160,000 troops to free Kuwait from Iraqi occupation.

Scud Attack

U.S. soldiers examine a
Scud shot down by a Patriot
missile in Saudi Arabia.

The biggest threats to Coalition forces, along with possible chemical attack, were Iraqi Scud missiles. These long-range missiles were developed by the Soviet Union during the Cold War. They were not very accurate, but they could be launched from mobile launchers, which were easy to hide. The Iraqis fired Scuds at Allied bases in Saudi Arabia, but most were shot down by Patriot missiles.

Saudi and U.S. military personnel examine the wreckage of a Saudi elementary school hit by a Scud missile in February 1991.

66 When the Scud attacks started… the sirens… went off every night, several times a night, until I guess the air-traffic controllers or the radar men became a little bit better at distinguishing what they were really looking for, we would have two or three alarms a night. (I) have never gotten dressed so fast in my life… If anybody wants to test me on putting on a chemical protective garment, we can all do it very quickly.

The going joke was, you know, 'What did you do in the war, Mommy?''Well, I got dressed in the middle of the night and jumped in a hole, because we had our bunkers built, and that was our defensive position, because the only defense against a Scud, or against what else might come out of it, was just to be properly dressed… 'We had one Scud that actually did get shot down… It looked like someone had set off firecrackers. 99

Captain Theresa O. Cantrell served in 32nd Medical Supply, Optical, and Maintenance Battalion, U.S. Army.

SCUD ATTACK FACTS

- The Soviet Union first used Scuds in the 1960s. The missiles had a range of up to 500 miles (800 km) and were fired from mobile launchers or static sites.
- The Scud had only a basic guidance system and was notoriously inaccurate.
- On February 25, 1991, a Scud strike on a U.S. Marine barracks near Dharhan killed 28 Marines and wounded about 150. This was one-fifth of all U.S. casualties during the war.
- The U.S. military claimed that its Patriot ground-to-air missiles destroyed 70 percent of Scud attacks, but such a high success rate is disputed.

Chemical Warfare

Iraq had used chemical weapons in its war with Iran from 1980 to 1988. Coalition commanders feared that Saddam Hussein would use Scud missiles to attack their troops with sarin, a poisonous gas. To defend against chemical attack, Coalition forces were issued with masks and protective clothing. They took tablets as a precaution against chemical weapons before any attack came, and had MARK 1 antidote kits that they would use afterward.

U.S. Marines in field protective masks take defensive positions on the perimeter of their camp.

66 My nightmare scenario was that our forces would attack into Iraq, and find themselves in such a great concentration that they became targeted by chemical weapons or some sort of a rudimentary nuclear device that would cause mass casualties.

That's exactly what the Iraqis did in the Iran/Iraq war. They would take the attacking masses of the Iranians, let them run up against their barrier system, and when there were thousands of people massed against the barrier system, they would drop chemical weapons and kill thousands of them…

There was every reason to believe that they would do [the same] opposing us. And we also knew that they had some limited nuclear capability, and thought that perhaps they could assemble some sort of very, very rudimentary device which they could detonate. **99**

Supreme UN commander, U.S. General Norman Schwarzkopf, discusses Coalition commanders' fear that Saddam might use chemical weapons against their troops.

CHEMICAL WARFARE FACTS

- Postwar inspections suggested that the Iraqis did not in fact use chemical weapons during the war.
- However, after the war as many as 250,000 Coalition soldiers suffered from "Gulf War Syndrome," a sickness experts believe may have been caused by chemical warfare.
- Scientists believe tiny amounts of poisonous chemicals may have been carried into Saudi Arabia by dust clouds.
- Chemical weapon detectors sounded alarms on Coalition bases, but they went off so frequently that soldiers often assumed they were false alarms.

Support staff wear protective clothing during a biological–chemical warfare drill in Saudi Arabia.

21

Air Attack

U.S. Marine Corps Harrier II attack aircraft fly over Saudi Arabia during Operation Desert Shield.

Before a ground offensive began, the Coalition carried out a six-week air offensive to knock out strategic and military targets. The aircraft included the new F-117 Stealth bomber, which could drop bombs without being detected. The Iraqi air force had Soviet MiG fighter-bombers, but limited its activities to patrolling rather than attacking the enemy.

An Iraqi munitions bunker lies in ruins after an Allied air strike during the bombing campaign.

" My targets were to be the Iraqi Air Force HQ building and a command bunker. Both of these were located in Baghdad and they were very close together. I think I had a time gap of one and a half minutes between drops…

What really stuck in my mind was coming up on the city. We were in the second wave to hit… By this time, they were mad and ready for us… I was about thirty minutes from the city and the visibility over the desert was phenomenal. In the back of my mind, I knew all the lights in Baghdad would be off, but for some reason they were on… at least that is what I thought. As I got closer, I realized that the lights were all ground-muzzle flashes from the Triple-A [antiaircraft artillery]! "

Major Rod "Hawkeye" Shrader (Bandit 312) of the 416th Squadron flew F-117 no 841 (nickname "Mystic Warrior") on the first night of the war and describes what it was like.

AIR WAR FACTS

- The first night of operations over Iraq (January 16/17, 1991) saw the longest ever bombing run. Seven B-52Gs took off from Louisiana, flew to Iraq, dropped their bombs, and flew back home.
- A total of 90,000 tons of bombs were dropped on Iraq.
- Aircraft from Britain, Bahrain, Canada, France, Italy, Kuwait, Qatar, Saudi Arabia, and the United Arab Emirates took part alongside the United States.
- The F-117 Stealth bomber could not be detected by Iraqi radar because of its radar-absorbent coating.

Sea Patrol

Four aircraft carriers and two guided missile cruisers of a U.S. battle force sail home from the Gulf.

Even before Iraq invaded Kuwait, the United States had eight warships stationed in the Persian Gulf to protect oil supplies. After the invasion, naval forces were the first Coalition forces to arrive. They supported the land and air campaigns. They fired missiles into Iraq and were a launch platform for warplanes.

“ Defence watches! It is like night during the day. In fact it has been like that for the last week or so. Constant night-time. When you are in eight-hour defence watches, you forget actually when it is day and when it is night. The fires that are ongoing on the Kuwait coastline you can see really clearly, orange just fills the skyline and the air is pungent with thick black oil and death.

Silkworms (Iraqi missiles) still operational according to the latest BDA [battle damage assessment]… so air raids are ordered yet again to blast away the suspected sites. B-52 bombers are tasked to do the job. They tell us when the raids will be… It's not a problem because you see the aircraft on your radar obviously going inland to do their business. The problem for me is when they have finished. They have a strict set, defined area of the coastline at which they must exit the battle area so we can tell they are friendly aircraft, but do they do it? NO! Some do but some don't. **”**

Mike Brodie was stationed on the Royal Navy air defence ship HMS *Exeter* in the Persian Gulf.

NAVAL WAR FACTS

- The U.S. Navy deployed six carrier battle groups to the Persian Gulf.
- Iraqi sea mines damaged two U.S. ships.
- The U.S. ships were armed with 1000-lb Tomahawk land attack missiles (TLAM).
- On the first day of Desert Storm, U.S. ships launched 122 Tomahawks, mainly on targets in Baghdad.
- Short-range fighter planes took off from and landed on aircraft carriers
- The U.S. Navy helped mislead Saddam into believing that an amphibious landing was likely from the sea.

U.S. personnel man a patrol craft in the Gulf in support of the ground invasion.

The Enemy

The Iraqi Army was largely made up of conscripts, but also included the elite Republican Guard, Sadam Hussein's bodyguards. Many were veterans of the eight-year war with Iran, which had ended in 1988. When the ground campaign began, however, it soon became clear that the Iraqis' equipment was inferior and their morale was low. Huge numbers of Iraqis surrendered without fighting at all.

Defeated Iraqi officers study a map to show their captors the location of military facilities inside Iraq.

An Iraqi troop leader shouts at his men as they drill in Baghdad in August 1990.

" Saddam Hussein is crazy and there can never be peace if he is alive… Now we have war against the whole world, not just the United States. Everyone knows we cannot win a war against the world. Everything that Saddam Hussein does is for war. Our people are not educated because they must serve in the army…

[Iraqis] are not like the Americans; we are not logical. We do not plan; we do not train. We may write on the training schedule that we train for three hours a day, but we do not really do this. On a busy day we might train for one hour, but not hard. They just told us to shoot to the last bullet and the last man. In the Iran–Iraq War, we would first shoot the artillery at the Iranians. Then the Iranians would charge our positions and we would shoot at them. If we did not hit them, they would be killed by our minefields. That is the Iraqis' idea of 'tactics.' "

Major Imad "B," commander of an Iraqi artillery battalion, being interviewed by U.S. military intelligence after his capture.

ENEMY FACTS

- At the start of the war, the Iraqi Army was the fourth largest in the world, with around 1.2 million soldiers, 5,800 tanks, 5,100 armored vehicles, and 3,850 artillery pieces.
- The United States helped arm Iraq during its eight-year war with Iran.
- The 12 units of the elite Republican Guard represented the most serious threat to Coalition forces.
- Iraqi conscripts had poor equipment and unreliable supplies; their morale was damaged by the Coalition air campaign.
- Mass desertion by Iraqi troops brought the war to a speedy end.

Special Forces

Before the ground war began, U.S. and British Special Forces teams were sent behind enemy lines into Iraq and Kuwait. They were mainly from the British SAS (Special Air Service) and U.S. Delta Force. Their job was to find out where enemy soldiers and vehicles were hidden. Some special forces teams stayed behind after the war to try and locate enemy weapons such as Scud missiles.

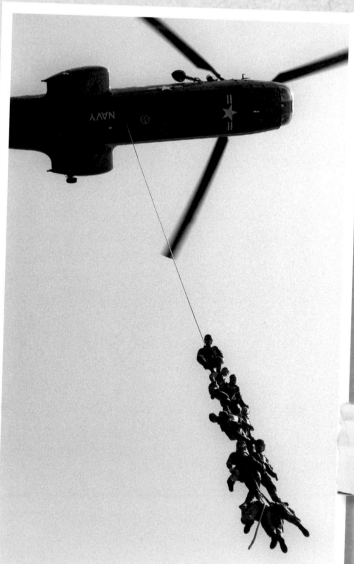

U.S. Navy SEALs and French commandos hang from a helicopter during a training exercise.

A member of the Special Forces searches an Iraqi trench for hidden enemy soldiers.

" When we got off the helicopters [inside Iraq], there were a lot of dogs barking and as the helicopter went away, there was a sort of a let down of everybody's heart, because they knew once that left, we were a hundred and fifty miles inside enemy territory. And there were no other forces around, that we were on our own…

It really didn't look very good for us. There's a hundred and fifty man element out there, and there's only eight of us with small arms. I can remember feeling, inside myself, my gosh, we're all going to die here. This is it, there's just too many soldiers. There's no way that we can get out of this… We then ended up in a fire fight that lasted the rest of the day, virtually up to, into the evening hours. **"**

Green Beret Commander Chad Balwanz and his team fought off 100 Iraqi soldiers and were rescued by a Black Hawk helicopter.

SPECIAL FORCES FACTS

- Approximately 10,000 troops, or about 10 percent of the total U.S. forces in action in the Gulf War, belonged to the Special Forces.
- Special Forces soldiers spoke Arabic and were invaluable for their language skills.
- Their tasks were confidential but are known to have included locating and assassinating key figures in Sadam Hussein's Ba'ath Party and sabotaging infrastructure such as electrical plants.
- U.S. Navy SEALs (Sea, Air, Land Teams) trained Kuwaiti commandos who took part in the liberation of Kuwait City.

Into Kuwait

U.S. Marines in light atmored vehicles arrive in Kuwait City after the Iraqi withdrawal.

The Coalition attack into Kuwait began on February 24, 1991, during a sandstorm that blinded both sides. It was a great success. U.S. Marines and Arab forces attacked Kuwait from the south; U.S. VII Corps attacked from the west as the 18th Airborne headed into Iraq before turning east through the Euphrates River valley. The Iraqi forces in Kuwait were encircled in just 100 hours.

" We were essentially the first Americans into Kuwait City… And the outpouring was something I'll never forget. I don't know where all the people came from… I mean there were thousands and thousands of Kuwaiti citizens still there, but they somehow sensed that we were driving through… and they came down to the side of the road, by the thousands.

They had Kuwaiti flags, and some had American flags. Some were crying. It was really chaotic. Vehicles that the Iraqis hadn't stolen, or destroyed, they had acquired some of those, so they were driving around us in this mad circle. I felt sure we were going to crush a vehicle. But what they were saying was, and not to make it too dramatic but it was, with tears streaming down their faces, what they were saying was, 'God bless you America, God bless you, we love you.' **"**

Lieutenant General Walt Boomer led the U.S. Marines in Desert Storm. His command were the first Americans into Kuwait City.

INTO KUWAIT FACTS

- Casualties were low during the invasion but friendly fire was a problem.
- The land war was the shortest part of the Gulf War, but military planners had always considered it the most risky part of the war.
- In the air and at sea the Coalition was far superior, but on the land it was more evenly matched with the Iraqi Army.
- The ground offensive began at 4.00 a.m. local time on February 24, 1991.
- The ground invasion used infantry and armor, but also Patriot missiles to intercept Scud missiles.

Civilians and soldiers in Kuwait wave flags in celebration on February 27, 1991, after the Iraqi retreat.

Desert Warfare

When the Coalition launched its ground assault on February 24, 1991, U.S. estimates suggested there might be as many as 400,000 Republican Guards waiting in the Iraqi and Kuwaiti deserts. The deserts were also defended by huge numbers of buried mines. In reality the campaign lasted barely 100 hours as Iraqi soldiers surrendered in great numbers.

A Marine in the desert sights a target with an M-249 squad automatic weapon (SAW) during Operation Desert Storm.

A Kuwaiti M-113 armored personnel carrier crosses a trench in the desert.

66 We were moving faster than expected and had very few casualties, so for us it was going real well. We also heard the reports of how other fronts were doing and they were all good… The next day we moved out at first light. The terrain changed dramatically: it was hilly with lots of small scraggly bushes and more camels. We went through a large Bedouin camp. I wonder what they were thinking as this division rolled through.

Our air troops found a bunch of enemy tanks, so we stopped for a couple of hours while we worked with air force to take them out… I can't describe the power that you feel when artillery goes off anywhere nearby. The earth shakes, your body vibrates, the sound is deafening. I watched as these rockets were being fired—coming right at me and over my head, hitting about 10 miles (16 km) to our front. 99

Captain Samuel Grady Putnam III, a surgeon with the 1/1 Cavalry Squadron, 1st Armored Division, describes the ground assault in a letter to his wife.

DESERT WARFARE FACTS

- Most of the ground campaign was fought in flat sandy or stony deserts.
- Daytime temperatures were very high (over 120°F/48°C). Soldiers had to drink lots of water to stay alert.
- Nighttime temperatures plunged, so soldiers needed warm clothes and plenty of blankets.
- The desert was a problem for vehicles and aircraft. Dust and small stones thrown up by exhausts and helicopter blades caused engines to break down.
- Frequent dust storms obscured visibility and made it difficult for soldiers to breathe properly.

Attack on the Oil Wells

Smoke from burning oil wells darkens the sky above the desert in February 1991.

With the war lost, Saddam Hussein ordered one final act as part of a scorched-earth policy to show his defiance of the Coalition. Iraqi troops set fire to more than 600 Kuwaiti oil wells. The fires were an ecological disaster. Thick smoke filled the skies and sticky black oil polluted the desert sands, killing wildlife. It took nine months, until November 1991, to finally extinguish the burning wells.

66 It wasn't until February 26 that the situation changed. I went out for [early prayers] and realized something was very different—the air was pitch black with the smell of diesel wafting in the air. I couldn't see the way in front of me and I had to stumble around in the dark until I found my way to the *masjid* [mosque]. Someone behind me said, 'Saddam withdrew last night.' We decided to investigate the situation first-hand.

Sunrise took longer than usual due to the excessive darkness caused by the burning oil fields, which puffed out immense clouds of smoke and then caused crude oil to rain everywhere. When we finally left, we discovered that the withdrawal was indeed real, albeit chaotic, and the army could be found on the highways wandering, looking to find their way back to Iraq. 99

A Palestinian named Yaser was living in Kuwait. He describes the scene after the departing Iraqis set fire to the oil wells.

OIL WELL FACTS

- Saddam Hussein ordered the burning of Kuwaiti oilfields out of spite rather than military strategy.
- The whole Gulf region was covered in thick black smoke.
- An estimated six million barrels of oil were lost every day, costing Kuwait up to $1.5 billion.
- The Iraqis laid mines in the areas around the oil wells, which had to be cleared before the fires could be put out.
- Privately contracted crews from the civilian oil industry eventually put out the fires.

The Road to Basra

Iraqi soldiers fled Kuwait City on the night of February 26/27. They headed toward Basra in any vehicle they could find. Coalition aircraft and U.S. soldiers destroyed up to 2,000 vehicles. The Iraqi vehicles were sitting ducks. Many men fled into the desert. The destruction led President Bush to decide to cease fighting the following day.

This destroyed Iraqi T-55 main battle tank on the Basra Road has been graffitied by Coalition troops.

" It was obvious from the prisoners we took that the Iraqis had suffered from a lack of medical care, food, water. Some of them were dehydrated. They hadn't eaten in days. Some of them were kids, thirteen, fourteen, fifteen years old. Some were old men, fifty, sixty. That bothered me. Sure it did.

And it bothered me when I picked up four or five dead Iraqi soldiers on the road over there. It's something you remember. I'll never forget what I saw on that road, ever. "

Captain Douglas Morrison, 1st Squadron, 4th Cavalry, describes his experiences on the Basra Road at the end of the war; the road became known as the "Highway to Hell."

ROAD TO BASRA FACTS

- Highway 80 was a six-lane highway between Kuwait and Iraq that Iraqi armor used to invade Kuwait in 1990.
- The Coalition attack on the retreating Iraqis was highly controversial. The column came to a standstill, so men could not escape.
- The precise number of Iraqi dead is not known, but may have been up to 600.
- More than 300 vehicles were abandoned, including 28 tanks.

Wrecked Iraqi vehicles line the Basra Road. The highway came to a standstill, and the vehicles were sitting ducks for the Coalition.

The Home Front

The Gulf War was the first major conflict since the end of the Cold War in 1989. Its successful outcome was an endorsement of the United Nations and a morale boost for many in the West, who believed it was a just campaign against an aggressor. Some antiwar protesters marched on Washington D.C. and other cities, but most Americans approved of President George Bush's handling of the war. If the Vietnam War was the first televised war, the Gulf War was the first 24-hour live war. Americans watched the war unfold from their living rooms.

Americans demonstrate against the war in New York City. Some people claimed the war was really fought for control of oil supplies.

Jordanians hold up pictures of Saddam Hussein during a protest against the war.

" The Gulf War was the first to be live from both sides—a unique moment in communications history. We not only had the American coalition side from press briefings and on-the-scene reports in the Gulf itself… but we also had it from the enemy side—the enemy capital in Baghdad. We were able to make regular reports to an international audience, and it made it very exciting for everyone…

The bombing of Baghdad and the ground war that followed were the first time in media history, not only when both sides of a war were covered fully, but a time when much of the coverage was live. The incredible spectacle of the Gulf War persuaded CNN and other TV organizations to cover successive events in the same way…. What we see is what some observers say is a cultural phenomenon of a 'mediathon' approach to news and information. This is what the Gulf War brought to the United States and to the world. "

Peter Arnett was a CNN reporter who broadcast live during the first night of the Coalition bombing of Baghdad. He reflects on the significance of the events in the context of television history.

HOME FRONT FACTS

- In March 1991, President Bush enjoyed a 91 percent approval rating for his handling of Operation Desert Storm.
- CNN broadcast the war live continuously.
- Americans could also see Saddam Hussein on television; this was the first time the enemy had directly addressed Americans during a conflict.
- TV coverage affected military decisions. After an airstrike on a bunker killed women and children, the Coalition reassessed its strategy.
- Many people considered the conflict a "just" war and antiwar demonstrations were generally limited.

Medicine and Nursing

The Gulf War was different from previous wars because it was mainly fought with missiles. There was little hand-to-hand combat, so there were few battlefield casualties. The feared biological and chemical weapons were not used. Instead, soldiers found the extreme heat and sandstorms damaged their health, and dehydration was one of the most serious problems.

Members of the 85th Combat Medical Unit carry a simulated casualty from a Black Hawk helicopter during an exercise.

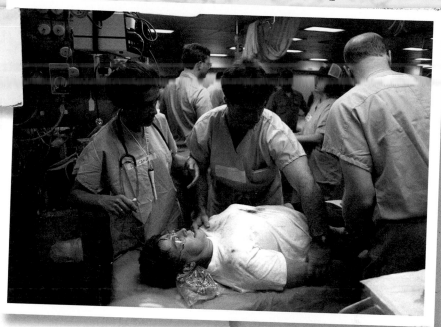

U.S. medical staff carry out a drill on board the hospital ship USNS Comfort in the Persian Gulf.

" We took care of our patients in the desert as we did at home. One thing I remember was the challenge of the Scud alerts and getting the patients out of the hospital into the bunker next to the hospital. Not all the patients could be removed from their equipment and taken to the bunkers.

We evacuated those patients that could be moved to the hospital bunker, but there were others that had to be left behind. The nurses stayed with their patients, protecting them as they could be with padding and assisting them with their gas masks. All alerts were considered to be real Scud attacks; therefore, these nurses and technicians were risking their lives for their patients… I would wonder when we would have injuries or symptoms displayed from a gas attack. But then we would hear the 'all clear,' and relief would set in and I realized it was fine once again. **"**

Jane Valentine served with the Air Force Nurse Corps as a lieutenant colonel with the 4th Medical Group.

NURSING FACTS

- Since returning from the Gulf, many veterans have suffered from a combination of medical problems known as 'Gulf War Syndrome.'
- The war zone was heavily contaminated with clouds of smoke and powdery wind-blown dust.
- Field hospitals had the latest medical equipment to deal with casualties.
- Most U.S. military physicians and nurses were called up from the reserves.
- Retired physicians were also called up to serve in the war, for the first time in more than 30 years.

Keeping Up Morale

During Operation Desert Shield, Coalition soldiers were unsure about what might happen when the fighting began. The nervousness harmed their morale. For many soldiers, boredom was also a problem. They played cards and board games, and wrote letters home. But the feelings of dread soon evaporated when Operation Desert Storm got underway. The speed of the victory led to widespread euphoria.

❝ It was very frustrating trying to get calls through to the States… We wondered if there were any phone booths at [the city of] Khamis… We went over there one night, real late, in the dark and parked the truck in front of a [phone booth]. We then dialled a certain 800 number. The next voice we heard was an AT&T operator in Atlanta!! We wanted to keep this setup quiet… We did, however, share the information with our flight commanders as this could be periodically used as a great tool for any of the pilots that were low in morale because they had not talked to their wives in a while….

I never knew when I was going to have time to call my wife …. Before I left for Saudi, I told her that if I ever called and left a number on her pager that was all sevens, she would know it was me and I was thinking about her. We kept this system going until I got back home! **❞**

Captain Scott Stimpert flew F-117 Stealth fighters on bombing raids from the start of Operation Desert Shield. Here he talks about how important a phone call home could be.

MORALE FACTS

- The constant false alarms warning of chemical attacks lowered morale.
- The hostile conditions in the desert also affected morale; 40 percent of troops became sick from local food and water.
- The hospitality and generosity of the Saudi civilians the soldiers met off base was another positive experience.
- President Bush visited the troops in Saudi Arabia on Thanksgiving Day, 1990.
- The United Service Organizations (USO) opened clubs in Saudi Arabia.
- Entertainers who performed for the troops included Jay Leno, Steve Martin, and Bob Hope on his final USO tour.

Bob Hope performs for the troops. Hope entertained troops in every war from World War II on.

Coming Home

On February 28, 1991, Saddam Hussein asked for a ceasefire. The air war had lasted for six weeks and the ground campaign for only a few days. Fighting continued sporadically, but the war had been limited, as President George Bush had promised. He did not send U.S. troops into Iraq to capture Baghdad or overthrow Saddam. Saddam remained the leader of Iraq. That was to cause more problems in the future.

U.S. Army flag bearers lead a Welcome Home parade through New York City on June 10, 1991.

66 The Day! We got up at 0630, packed, and cleared our billets. Then we bussed to the Green Ramp… We loaded our bags onto the hauler. The process got downright rowdy, with some of the junior officers flinging bags out of the bus. We howled with laughter, though we'd have been furious if anybody else treated our bags that way…

Two KC-135's arrived at 1130… We lifted off at 1230. On the way I got to ride for a bit in the [refueling] boom bay and look straight down, an amazing view. We did a flyby over the airport, then landed. When both planes were down, they opened the doors and we saw a huge crowd. We fell in behind the color guard, took a few steps, and somebody yelled 'Here they come.' That was the last time anything remotely resembled a military formation. The crowd rushed us. 99

Steven Dutch was a reservist in 432nd Civil Affairs Company, which helped Kuwait recover after the war. He describes returning home on June 19, 1991.

END OF THE WAR FACTS

- The ceasefire came into effect at midnight on February 28, 1991.
- American casualties stood at 148 battle dead and 145 nonbattle dead. The British lost 24, the French 2, and Arab nations 39.
- Iraqi casualties were around 100,000 dead, 300,000 wounded, 150,000 deserted, and 60,000 captured.
- Iraq accepted the United Nations terms for a ceasefire on April 6, 1991.
- The war was widely considered to be a success because of the remarkably low numbers of Coalition casualties.

GLOSSARY

amphibious An operation that takes place on land and sea.

armor Heavily defended weapons, such as tanks.

biological weapon A weapon that uses infectious agents, such as germs, to spread sickness or death.

bunker A reinforced underground shelter.

chemical weapon A weapon that uses missiles or other means to deliver chemicals that cause severe harm or death.

coalition A temporary alliance of countries or other groups that is formed to take combined action.

conscript Someone who has been forced to serve in the military.

deployment The distribution of armed forces ready for war.

friendly fire Weapons fire that accidentally kills forces who are fighting on the same side.

Gulf War Syndrome A medical condition suffered by many veterans of the war, with symptoms including fatigue, bad headaches, and breathing problems.

infrastructure The structures and facilities on which a society depends, such as roads and bridges.

inoculation A vaccination that prevents a disease.

logistics The task of housing and supplying troops to enable them to carry out an operation.

morale How positive or negative a person or group feels about achieving a particular task.

sanctions A penalty inflicted on a country, usually by limiting its trade.

stealth Technology that makes it difficult for an aircraft to be detected by radar or sonar.

strategic Related to the overall progress of a war rather than to the immediate outcome of a battle.

FURTHER INFORMATION

Books

Bingham, Jane. *The Gulf Wars With Iraq* (Living Through). Heinemann-Raintree, 2012.

Gitlin, Martin. *Operation Desert Storm* (Essential Events). Abdo Publishing Company, 2009.

Gregory, Josh. *The Persian Gulf War* (Cornerstones of Freedom). Scholastic, 2011.

Miller, Mary. *The Brave Women of the Gulf War* (Women at War). 21st Century Publishing, 2006.

Samuels, Charlie. *Machines and Weaponry of the Gulf War* (Machines that Won the War). Gareth Stevens Publishing, 2013.

Zwier, Lawrence J., and Matthew Scott Weltig. *The Persian Gulf and Iraqi Wars* (Chronicle of America's Wars). Lerner Publishing Group, 2004.

Websites

http://www.desert-storm.com/
A site maintained by veterans that contains a range of information about the Gulf War.

http://www.history.com/topics/persian-gulf-war
History.com guide with links to many articles about the war.

http://www.pbs.org/wgbh/pages/frontline/gulf/
PBS site to accompany the series *Frontline*.

news.bbc.co.uk/2/hi/middle_east/861164.stm
A brief timeline of the Gulf War from the BBC.

INDEX